NATURE INTO ART
— Designing With Our Planet

NATURE INTO ART

— Designing With Our Planet

Allan Howze – James Moretz

Flowerian Publishers • Chicago, Illinois

Nature invites curiosity and anticipation. It demands attention.
Man partakes.

NATURE INTO ART
–Designing With Our Planet

Produced by Allan Howze and James Moretz
Edited by Darren DeMatoff
Graphic Design by Bark Design, Chicago, IL
Photography by James Moretz and Allan Howze

ISBN 0-9670684-0-1

Published in 1999 by Flowerian Publishers, Chicago, IL

Printed and bound in Taipei, Taiwan, R.O.C.
by Cabin Printing, Ltd.

To order, contact:
American Floral Art School
529 South Wabash Avenue
Suite 610
Chicago, IL 60605-1679, USA
312.922.9328

Gold Leaf Design Group, Inc.®
337 North Oakley Boulevard
Chicago, IL 60612-2215, USA
312.738.1790
fax 312.738.1795
www.goldleafdesigngroup.com

©

FOREWORD... *Foreword*

Nature Into Art

Nature Into Art – Designing With Our Planet is a contemporary guide illustrating the relationship between nature and art.

The world is a melting pot of many elements and principles. These laws of nature are visual guides that help us not only to add ornamentation, but also to survive. Without nature, there would be no art, no man, no life. In every art form, the laws of nature are never far beneath the surface. From Stone-Age man, to early Native American Indian, to present day modern man, nature has prevailed. Man only mirrors nature. Nature has been recorded in every type of art form. It is our wish to help kindle this awareness of these relationships as well as an understanding of the source of all design and share it with all.

My affinity with nature began at a very early age. Being drawn to nature as a medium of expression seems only natural for me. This observance has been one of the most powerful teaching tools. I constantly look to the images of nature to learn compassion and an understanding for art and for life.

I wish to show my appreciation to those who have helped me reach a higher plane of thinking and comprehending: my parents who are MY architects, my family, and numerous friends. To James Moretz, I appreciate you immensely. Your friendship, your guidance and your unselfish giving reflects how humankind should respect others. Jim has candidly expressed to me numerous times, "It's not easy birthin' a book!" Even though this project has been a strenuous and never-ending journey, the experiences and knowledge gained will remain with me forever.

The world is in constant change…from year to year, millennium to millennium. It inspires us to seek new adventures. Hopefully, with self observation and an awareness of the world around us, we can all live a richer life; a life that nature has imprinted within us all. For nature is the true teacher. Nature is art, art is nature.

–Allan Howze

CHAPTER 1...

Chapter 1

...within us. From birth to death we all follow a normal and natural cycle "The Circle Of Life."

"The Circle Of Life."

...ly occurring earth bowls dot our world. The mystic architectural caverns of the Grand Canyon are formed by water. Craters are...

CIRCLE OF LIFE — *LESSONS FROM NATURE*

CHAPTER 5...CIRCLE OF LIFE

Every element of nature lies within us. From birth to death, we all follow a normal and natural cycle – "The Circle Of Life."

Naturally occurring earth bowls dot our world. The mystic architectural caverns of the Grand Canyon were formed by water. Craters are formed from asteroids bombarding the earth's surface. Fertile valleys are formed from volcanos that link the interior of the earth with the surface world. Pools in caves are formed from the slow painstaking drips of water from the ceiling hitting the hard surface of rock below. All are examples of Nature's earth bowls. In every instance, an outside force helps to create these natural bowls of life. Within each, sub-ecosystems are formed and flourish.

The earth bowls that were created on the following pages are an extension of observations from around the world. The earth bowls are not only expressions of artistry, but also scientific observations. These earth bowls were designed within two categories- season and geography. These categories determine both the setting and materials used in each bowl. The common denominator and starting point of all earth bowls is "Mother Earth."

In the end, it became even more clear how the earth is the supportive beginning for life on this planet. Scars on the earth's surface caused by the forces of nature- fire, floods, glaciers, man- all heal with time. Nature repairs itself. Nature is a "CIRCLE OF LIFE."

SPRING promise and renewal

SUMMER heat and passion

AUTUMN shades and abundance

WINTER celebration and death

TROPICAL   The rainforests emanate a sense of age and endurance;
            of peaceful life and tranquil death.

DESERT The sands journey across the earth's surface like nomads withstanding the test of time.

S E A S I D E A life source of minerals and elements that provide tranquility and rejuvenation for future generations.

F O R E S T

We live in a world filled with material goods; we are protected from the elements in our safe cocoon of concrete, glass and steel. Something is missing. Only when we escape the artificial environment, do we recognize how strong our human need is for contact with the natural world. There, we find our roots, our place in the scheme of things. There, we find energy...for the soul.

Nature has a beauty, that, if you let it, will change you.

CHAPTER 2 ...

chapter 2

ALTERNATIVE INSPIRATIONS
–DIVINE INTERVENTION

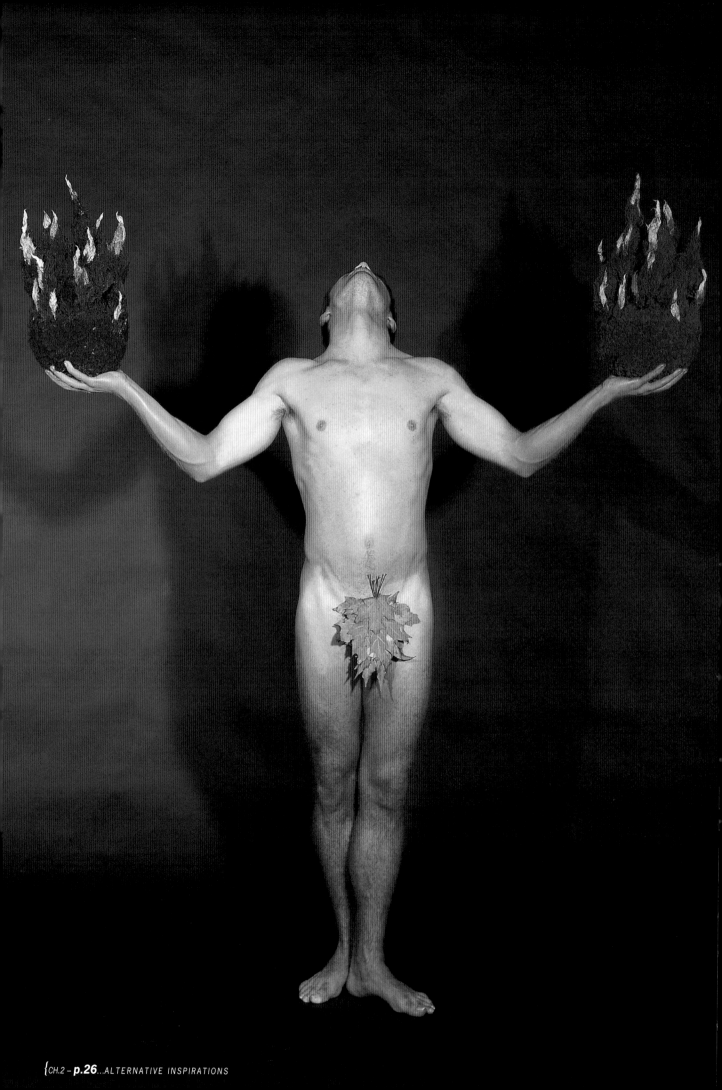

Arms painted green. Burgundy cockscomb spheres. Flames of burgundy and yellow <u>Celosia</u>. *14" diameter*

Planted fabric sculptures. *15' high x 3' wide*

Recycled dyed turkey feathers. *36" diameter*

Fresh bamboo, tied. *40' high x 40' wide.* Spheres of <u>Magnolia</u> <u>grandiflora</u> leaves, moss, red clay. *24" diameter each*

Organic structure lying in summer grass. 28" wide x 30" high x 50" long

Same structure with cottonwood seeds. 28" wide x 30" high x 50" long

Organic structures. Bound growing grass with clear string.
28" wide x 6.5' high

Structures cut from underneath then moved to a dry location.

Structures after two weeks. *August, 1997*

Fresh cattails and sunflowers.

Cocoons of mixed water weeds and
algae. *3' long*

Freestanding lilac stems with dyed, skeletonized magnolia leaves. *3' high x 2' wide*

Summer weeds.
4' high x 28" wide

Gemini. *18" wide x 12" high*

Gemini. *5' wide x 2' high*

Gemini. *4' wide x 18" high*

Pavé. Plant materials floating in water.
18" diameter each

Impressionistic vase by Ms. Kerri Buxton.
– Buxton/Taylor Studio – *Salt Lake City, Utah*

Weaving of jute and cattail foliage. Flowers
suspended with water source behind.
5' high x 4' wide

Webbing. Gold bullion. *32" high*

Fresh bear grass bundle, brass wire, star fruit.
20" high x 24" wide

Fresh bear grass bundle, brass wire,
cranberry sphere.
20" high x 24" wide

Branches, lichen, moss. *4' diameter x 4' high*

Calla, <u>Cryptanthus</u>, colored string.
12" diameter

Stop and remember you are walking on a world.

CHAPTER 3 *chapter 3*

Our planet displays a dr

Important building blocks intertwine to make up everythin
the same shape and 6.3 % larger than the last chamber
a bee's honeycomb always have 120° angles that make a

Every animate and inanimate object on our planet exempli
exists in everything we see, touch, smell, hear and taste.

Our planet displays ... living Force that creates and manages. Taking note of
world filled with ... structures of precision is the first step for lear...
...ing. Seeing is believ...

Important tool... ...e to make up everything in our world. T...
spiraling strands ... ...ngle cell evolving into a living being...
remarkable. Ca... ...lus shell is exactly the same shape a...
0.5 % larger ... ...manufactured by this incredible anim...
Delicate bran... ...crystals radiate into complex geometric
patterns. The ... ...of a bee's honeycomb always cut 1...
angles that make ... Nature creates order for survival and wit...
the least amount ... ...d. Overall, there is a strong force that is
...charge of our world.

that creates and manages. Taking note ... world filled with remarkable structures of precision is the first step for learning. Seeing is believ...

Every animate and ... animate object on our planet exemplifies a combination o...

world. The spiraling strands ... ...ngle cell creating into a living being is remarkable. Each chamber of the nautilus shell is exac... ...ed by this incredible animal. Delicate ... ...structure of ice crystals radiate into complex geometric patterns. The repeated wax chambers ... a city. Nature creates order for survival and with the least amount of energy expended. Overall, there is a strong force that is in charge of ...

We observe how a combination of elements ... elements into a working order, develops principles. Man has written the eleme...

ELEMENTS AND PRINCIPLES OF DESIGN
EXERCISING CREATIVITY

...ments and principles of design on paper. Nature displays the laws in every
...nation of characteristics that help us to understand its construction. These rules (Elements and Principles) help us to understand the order t...
...eason for everything. We observe how a combination of elements make up an object. Putting those elements into a working order, develops prin...
aspect of its existen...
...ples. Man has written the elements and principles of design on paper. Nature displays the laws in every aspect of its existen...

Elements are tangible, working ingredients which are used to create. In th...
Elements are tangible, working ingredients which are used to create. In this chapter we examine these elemen...
chapter we examine these el...
Line, Shape, Form, Texture, Color and Spa...
Line, Shape, Form, Texture, Color and Spac...

Principles are intangible rules that help develop functions. We will observe these princip...
Principles are intangible rules that help develop functions. We will observe
these princ...

Exercising Creativity

Our planet displays a driving **FORCE** that creates and manages. Taking note of a world filled with remarkable structures of precision is the first step for learning. Seeing is believing.

Important building blocks intertwine to make up everything in our world. The spiraling strands of DNA within a single cell evolving into a living being is remarkable. Each chamber of the nautilus shell is exactly the same shape and 6.3 % larger than the last chamber manufactured by this incredible mollusk. Delicate branching structures of ice crystals radiate into complex geometric patterns. The repeated wax chambers of a bee's honeycomb always have 120° angles that make a home into a city. Nature creates order for survival and with the least amount of energy expended. Overall, there is a strong force that is in charge of our world.

Every animate and inanimate object on our planet exemplifies a combination of characteristics that help us to understand its construction. These rules (Elements and Principles) help us to understand the order that exists in everything we see, touch, smell, hear and taste. There is a reason for everything. We observe how a combination of elements make up an object. Putting those elements into a working order develops principles. Man has written the elements and principles of design on paper. Nature displays the laws in every aspect of its existence.

Elements are tangible, working ingredients which are used to create. In this chapter we examine these elements: **Line, Shape, Form, Texture, Color and Space.**

Principles are intangible rules that help develop functions. We will observe these principles: **Pattern, Order, Repetition, Dominance, Balance, Rhythm, Harmony, Size, Proportion and Scale.**

The Elements and Principles of design are intertwined. For example, a parrot's plumage has beautiful color. Physically, the parrot can have any color of feather. It is not directly dependent on the element of color to exist. The principles of design are what is needed to construct the parrot so that it may fly, sing, eat, etc. The element of color does play a role in the parrot's survival, however. It provides camouflage and helps attract a mate. The relationship of these natural Elements and Principles can be witnessed in every form on this planet. The laws of nature are never far beneath the surface. Nature's classroom evokes artistry and science.

Line. A line forms a path for the eye to follow in a composition. Lines are connecting tools within a design. The primary types of lines are vertical, horizontal, diagonal and curved. Lines form branching patterns.

Shape. A flat outline or silhouette which has two dimensions. See form.

Form. A three dimensional shape that has substance. It occupies space and has depth (not to be confused with a shape which is a flat outline or silhouette).

Three shapes that are the beginning of all forms and are considered to be perfect:

- **Circle** It represents continual motion. It gives a feeling of relaxation and the gathering of force *(circle of friends)*. A sphere, the three dimensional expression of the circle, is thought of as a heavenly body exhibiting power, control and influence.

- **Triangle** It appears sharp and aggressive *(majestic mountains)*. Its visual weight appears lighter than the other shapes. A pyramid is a polyhedron that has triangular faces while having four sides.

- **Square** Perfectly balanced, it appears heavy and hard; and, forms right angles *(squared away, a slang for balanced)*. A cube has six square (equal) sides, twenty right angles and can stand alone on any of its sides.

Texture. The physical surface structure of a substance, which helps to give a third dimension in design.

Color. The effect of varying qualities of light reflected from a surface.

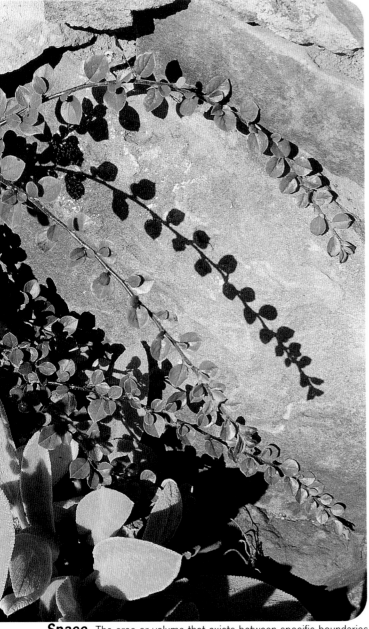

Space. The area or volume that exists between specific boundaries. It is the format of all design.

- **Positive Space.** The area occupied by an image or a dimensional object.

- **Negative Space.** The area that is unoccupied by an image or dimensional object. The emptiness which makes a contribution to a design.

Pattern. A composite of lines, forms, colors and the spaces between them that occur again and again. Patterns have rhythm and exemplify repetition. Repetition does not always show pattern. Compared to all other elements and principles, we probably notice pattern more.

Order. A governing condition which dictates the physical aspects, placement and function of the elements of design. –*Unity.*

Repetition. One component displaying the same qualities more than once. Repetition is the element in pattern.

Dominance. The distinct difference between
the importance of materials in a composition.
–*Accent.*

Balance. An influence or force (physical force or visual force) tending to produce equilibrium or stability. Eastern countries have mastered the art of asymmetry, while Western countries have become accustomed to symmetry.

- **Symmetrical Balance.** Equal visual weight on either side of an imaginary line that bisects the composition.

- **Asymmetrical Balance.** Unequal visual weight on either side of an imaginary line that bisects the composition.

- **Open Balance.** In many new styles of design, when the distinct characteristics of either symmetrical or asymmetrical balance are not evident.

PRINCIPLES

Rhythm. A regularly recurring element that moves the eye from one point to another in a composition (organized visual movement of individual parts).

Harmony. The study of relationships. It shows unity between elements working together.

Size. The dimension of a line, shape, form or space.

Proportion. A comparative relationship between quantities or qualities of elements within a design.

Scale. A comparison, usually with size, between a design and its setting.

Nature provides the setting. It creates the mood. It evokes a response.

CHAPTER 4 ...

chapter 4

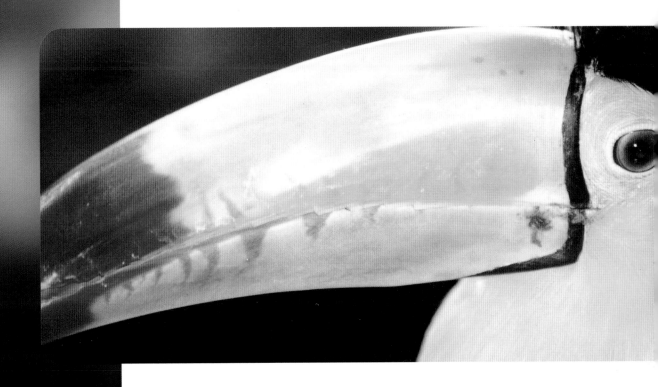

LIVING COLORS – *A SPECTRUM OF LIGHT*

Yellow sparkles atop blue drifting waters that run forever into the sun. Moody greys of shadows creeping up to mountaintops. Clear white beams of light penetrating green leaves like stained glass in a cathedral. Brittle browns of over-matured leaves lying on the forest floor. The colors of nature create a setting, a backdrop to our world. Colors inspire moods and evoke responses. They are the emotions in our design world. Colors define our seasons and dictate our feelings.

If color is such a natural and instinctive part of our lives, why are so many people afraid of using color in design? Nature is a great teacher. Take note of the many different color combinations that are in our natural world. It's not hard to see that many color combinations exist before our eyes.

Color attracts and color detracts. Many of the colorful birds and butterflies of the rainforests flaunt bright palettes of colors for protection as well as attraction. Numerous tree frog species in these same forests display bright "neon-like" markings to frighten predators and to warn of their toxicity. From good to bad, there is a reason for everything. From camouflaging to flaunting, color helps the world go around. Color is intangible. It has the strength to make one visualize and to sense. In design, color must be considered scientifically, artistically and psychologically.

"Elephante" artist Michael Kahn, Cornville, AZ.
Found colored glass.

Light.
The source of all color.
Light can be separated into a spectrum of different colors. This is the
foundation for our man-made color wheel.

Light can be broken into an array, a spectrum, of hues (colors). Colors are created by light. No light, no color! Light quality and light quantity can change the intensity (chroma) of the colors dramatically.

The color wheel is a man-made system of arranging the color spectrum. By connecting the opposite ends of the spectrum, a circle or wheel is formed.

The presence and/or absence of color can enhance or detract from a design. Color is the spice that adds emotion to design. Nature gives the artist a vast palette of hues or colors to utilize. Hue is the technical term given to any color. Tints, tones and shades are different variations (values) of a hue made by adding white, grey or black, respectively. Value denotes the lightness or darkness of a hue. Red, yellow and orange hues create warm feelings; blue, violet and green hues create cool feelings.

Primary hues are the beginning of all colors (red, yellow, blue). They are the most true of all colors. Secondary hues (orange, green, violet) are developed by combining two primary colors together in equal quantities. Tertiary hues are developed by combining one primary hue together with one secondary hue in equal amounts. The most simple groupings of colors create schemes or themes, and are explained as monochromatic, analogous and complementary.

Monochromatic is a family of different tints, tones, and shades of a single hue. An analogous family is made of a combination of neighboring colors within a 90 degree angle on the color wheel. A complementary family is composed of hues that are opposite each other on the color wheel.

Interestingly, the color wheel displays an ongoing, continuous cycle. One color always leads to another color. From primary, secondary and tertiary hues to monochromatic, analogous and complementary color schemes, our color wheel appropriately describes our colorful world as we know it. According to the determined placement of colors in the color wheel, we can see that nature is only imitated in this circular pattern.

Again, another continuous circle of life.

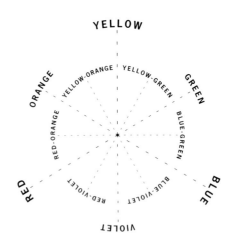

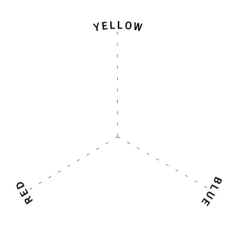

YELLOW

RED   BLUE

Primary Hues. RED, YELLOW, BLUE - the beginning of all colors.

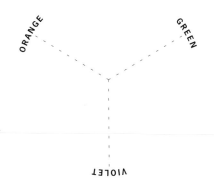

ORANGE   GREEN

VIOLET

Secondary Hues. ORANGE, GREEN, VIOLET - made by combining equal amounts of two primary colors.

YELLOW-ORANGE   YELLOW-GREEN

RED-ORANGE   BLUE-GREEN

RED-VIOLET   BLUE-VIOLET

Tertiary Hues. RED-ORANGE, YELLOW-ORANGE, YELLOW-GREEN, BLUE-GREEN, BLUE-VIOLET, RED-VIOLET -made by combining a primary hue with a secondary hue in equal quantities.

Hue. The technical term given to any **color.**

Tint. A hue that is made by adding white.

Tone. A hue that is made by adding grey.

Shade. A hue that is made by adding black.

Green
A secondary hue that is formed from adding together the primary colors of blue and yellow.
It is the neutral and dominating color in nature.

Warm Hues
REDS, YELLOWS, ORANGES – Advancing colors that have the psychological effect of warmth because of their association with the sun or fire.

Cool Hues
BLUES, GREENS, VIOLETS – Receding colors that have a calming effect and are associated with green leaves, water and ice.

Monochromatic
A family of different tints, tones and shades of a single hue that are related to each other on the color wheel.

Complementary
A family of "unrelated" colors that lie opposite each other on the color wheel.

RED & GREEN
RED-ORANGE & BLUE-GREEN
ORANGE & BLUE
YELLOW-ORANGE & BLUE-VIOLET
YELLOW & VIOLET
YELLOW-GREEN & RED-VIOLET

Analogous
A family of "related" colors on the color wheel that lie within a 90 degree angle.

RED, RED-ORANGE, ORANGE, YELLOW-ORANGE
RED-ORANGE, ORANGE, YELLOW-ORANGE, YELLOW
ORANGE, YELLOW-ORANGE, YELLOW, YELLOW-GREEN
YELLOW, YELLOW-GREEN, GREEN, BLUE-GREEN
YELLOW-GREEN, GREEN, BLUE-GREEN, BLUE
GREEN, BLUE-GREEN, BLUE, BLUE-VIOLET
BLUE-GREEN, BLUE, BLUE-VIOLET, VIOLET
BLUE-VIOLET, VIOLET, RED-VIOLET, RED
VIOLET, RED-VIOLET, RED, RED-ORANGE
RED-VIOLET, RED, RED-ORANGE, ORANGE

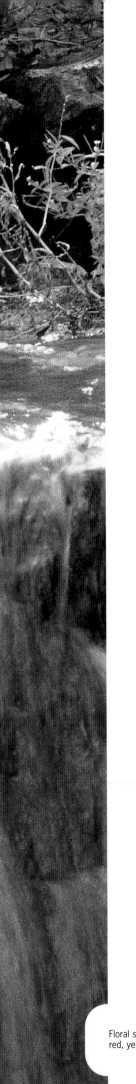

Nature provides a stage for all to be seen.

Floral spheres of the primary colors,
red, yellow and blue.

CHAPTER 5 ... *chapters 5*

Designing is a basic human act and knowingly or not all artists look to nature as a guide for design, and for aesthetic inspiration. Man's intervention with nature has been a continuous relationship of necessity and creativity.

chapter, we illustrate the human urge to bring nature closer to our daily lives. We use natural elements to adorn the architecture of our buildings, our clothing,

NATURE INTO ART
– BRIDGING DESIGN WITH MOTHER NATURE

Designing is a basic human act. Knowingly or not, all artists look to nature as a guide for design, and for aesthetic inspiration. Man's intervention with nature has been a continuous relationship of necessity and creativity.

In this chapter, we illustrate the human urge to bring nature closer to our daily lives. We use natural elements to adorn the architecture of our buildings, our clothing, our furniture. We also surround our buildings with formal gardens. Natural scenes are the focus of many paintings and sculptures. In addition to this need of being close to nature, we examine the natural laws that permeate our design.

Shapes and forms imitate the natural world of humans, animals and plants. Fruit and vegetable forms have been repeated by glassblowers, potters and metalworkers for centuries in many civilizations. In ancient times, necessity dictated the forming of utilitarian objects. Using nature as inspiration, these "necessary" objects were decorated to show possession and to celebrate the appreciation of the environment around them. This led to the creation of objects that were purely decorative, still using nature's laws and inspiration.

Nature and Architecture

— Architecture is a familiar part of our everyday lives. It displays the marriage of geometrical science and nature. Numerous natural forms occur frequently in our architectural decorations. Nature is displayed in almost every building, in one form or another. It is a well-known fact that most plant and animal forms were, at one time, associated with mythological gods and had symbolic meanings; usually, with death and the afterlife. For example, a wreath of laurel branches was the highest honor and reward given at the ancient Olympic Games. It also symbolizes wisdom in Greek mythology. In both pagan and Christian arts, the laurel wreath symbolizes peace. The most recognized and frequently occurring natural form in classical decoration is the acanthus plant (Acanthus mollis and Acanthus spinosa).

A simple observation of architecture will reveal other types of flora. The most commonly used floras are olive branches, ivy vines and tendrils, oak leaves and branches, acorns, pomegranates, bellflowers, pine branches and cones, thistle, lilies, ginkgo, ferns, lotus, and mixtures of fruit. The animal and insect world are also an important element in design. Both flora and fauna contribute to the design world. Some examples of fauna commonly found are the dragonfly, bee, bat, scarab, chameleon, dolphin, swallow, nautilus and other shells, sea horse, snake, ram, monkey, lion, dove and horse. Examples of mythical characters include gargoyles, Greek gods and goddesses, dragons and cherubs.

Nature seems to delight in the creation of varied geometric shapes and forms (see chapter 3). The most revered are the circle/sphere and the square/cube. These geometric forms suggest stability and order and are the basis for the majority of our designs. A square is a shape; a cube is a form. A circle is a shape; a ball (sphere) is a form. Each is said to have mystical properties and is found in every civilization since the beginning of time. Geometric shapes dominate our constructed environment. They're evident in buildings, furniture, industrial design and floral design.

Nature and Gardens – In the French garden, nature was confined to

strict forms of geometry and logic. Topiaries were formal expressions of power and control; the more ornate the garden, the wealthier the person. Overwhelming flauntings are noted with the Sun King, Louis XIV, and in the gardens of Versailles. Gardens were coveted as representations of control. Symmetry and balance were common denominators with landscape architecture and architecture in the mid 1600s. Interior and exterior architecture displayed lavish fruit and floral motifs. Gold gilded festoons of fruit adorned the exteriors, round flower medallions lined the ceilings, Acanthus leaves bordered the mirrors and doorways, and floral bouquets and garlands were embedded into tapestries and carpets. Pools of water reflected the painted colors of the trees. Flora and fauna were designed into stone urns and bronze water fountains. Today, we can still take note of the strong, strict practice of controlling nature. Texture and form are dramatic combinations for unconventional means of artistic natural art expressions. As one can see, we depend upon nature for support, nourishment, beauty and healing. Nature is treated as the architecture of our souls.

Nature and Lines

– In nature, there are four universal ways in which lines are related. They are: lines traveling in the same direction (parallelism), traveling in opposite directions (opposition), starting from a common point (radiation) or traveling in all directions (confusion). The first three groups of lines are associated with universal natural laws representing perfection in order, as opposed to chaos, represented by the last group. Most floral designers would be surprised at the idea that they don't actually arrange the flowers, *but* arrange the flowers' stems. The inflorescence (flowers) attached to the stems merely follow the pattern established by the stems or lines.

As seen in nature, trees illustrate these four ways of positioning lines. A forest or jungle exhibits "lines of confusion" with a tangle of confused lines. Several trees, growing side by side, show "lines of parallelism". The horizontal earth is in direct contrast or at right angles to upright trees, depicting "lines of opposition". A single tree depicts "lines of radiation" in two directions. Roots and root hairs radiate downward into the soil in search of water and nutrients. Branches radiate upward in search of sunlight and carbon dioxide in the process of producing their own food through photosynthesis.

To a lesser degree, these four universal ways of relating lines may be compared to the four seasons of the year: Winter (confusion) – the weight of the snow and ice bending and breaking shrubs and trees; Spring (parallelism) – new growth sprouting side by side and straight up from the ground; Summer (radiation) – flowers, plants and trees' roots fanning out upward and downward for light, air, water and nutrients; Autumn (opposition) – the vertical growth of barren trees silhouetted against the horizon or reflected in the peaceful blue water of a lake or pond.

Lines of Parallelism – Lines that have the same direction, course or tendency are said to be parallel. The term is derived from the Greek word 'parallelos' meaning beside one another.

In floral design, the lines (flower stems) are placed parallel to each other vertically, horizontally or diagonally. Parallel designs have roots in both ikebana landscape designs and the Egyptian columns of flowers. The flower's stems are placed in two or more groupings in a vertical pattern with space between the groups. Parallelism is a general floral design category that is subdivided into several styles. These styles include vegetative, landscape, botanical, hedge row (garden wall) and Biedermeier (See Chapter 6).

Lines of Opposition – Lines going in an opposite direction have a relationship based on one of the universal laws called "opposition". In the plant world, opposition of vertical and horizontal elements is expressed with many flowers and other parts of the plant. For example, a freesia or Easter lily (<u>Lilium</u> <u>longiflorum</u>) is at a right angle to the flower's stem. The principle of 'two' predominates in life—large-small, male-female, tall-short, night-day, God-man, heaven-earth, good-evil and the yin-yang symbol. Primitive man often thought in terms of duality but introduced dissimilarities for variety and for creativity. 'Opposites attract' states the old adage that can result in many of the joys or sorrows of life. When in harmony with each other, opposites can be creative and energetic; but, when not in harmony, this opposition can be boring or non-functional. The symbol of the Christian cross, with its lines of opposition, has several connotations. The relationship of this symbol to the human figure is self-evident. The theologian may see the vertical line representing man's aspirations with the horizontal line being symbolic of his earthly existence.

This opposition involves the law of balance. The well-known psychologist, Abraham Maslow, noted that the mature and well-developed personality tends to combine seemingly opposite approaches, just as the yin-yang symbol suggests. In doing so, a person creates a synergy that makes movement through change easy and graceful. The balance is not always symmetrical, but it is a balance of two unlike objects that offers more challenging design possibilities. Lines of opposition involve contrasting lines balanced with a common focal area, as seen in the L-shaped arrangement in floral design. A series of L-shaped designs, in one arrangement, results in the New Convention style. It is typical of the vertical and horizontal lines of a city's skyline. Lines of opposition are evident in fabric construction. Vertical and horizontal (warp and weft) fibers are woven to become a solid sheet.

Lines of Radiation – Lines

starting from a common point are found in much of nature. "Straight, curved, bent or broken lines may be arranged so that they appear to start from one given point. Life constantly starts from a point and fans outward in all directions" (Bates, *Basic Design*). This is seen in the examples of a spider web, a single tree with roots and branches, exploding fireworks, the luminous Rose Window of the Notre Dame Cathedral in Paris, and the geographical patterns of streets radiating into the famous buildings and monuments in Washington, DC.

Radiation is the most common and important way of arranging flower stems in commercial floral design as well as other types of floral design (ikebana, garden club). In a one-sided design, all stems come from a central focal area. Usually there is a strong focal point flower placed at the top, front, and center of the container. In an all-around design, the stems radiate from the center. Our "formal" floral designs all display the laws of nature. These arrangements have flower stems that appear to radiate from one point as most plants do naturally. We associate with designing in this manner only because it is the normal thing to do. Humans have been imitating nature since the birth of man.

Nature has never been content with simple shapes, but has created all kinds of intricate mathematical designs. Instead of being interested in a whole landscape or view, an artist may study a natural object up close, such as a shell. The spiraling growth habit of the shell is based on the "golden proportion." The spiral has a mathematical consistency and can be found in numerous other examples displayed in nature. We are connected more strongly to nature than we will ever realize or admit. In the 13th century, Leonardo Pisana (Fibonacci) hinted at the interaction of proportions with a direct and measurable connection between beauty and mathematics. This proportional relationship is seen in nature and in the creations of man. Man seems by instinct to prefer forms that follow strict mathematical rules. The dimensions used on a standard postcard or the standard 9' x 15' room are not just happy accidents.

Lines of Confusion

Lines of Confusion – At times, artists have distorted nature's appearance to pass on some special feeling they may have about nature itself. Abstract shapes are distorted natural shapes. The source of the shape is recognizable, but it's not depicted in a realistic manner. A few Asian ikebana schools, contemporary garden club designs and today's free form and abstract designs use flower stems or branches in a controlled but crossing manner. "Lines may go in any direction but still have a fascinating sense of order. Adhering to the rules of design too closely produces an unimaginative and sterile quality. The designs we make are either pleasing or not. An explanation is unnecessary. If art can be explained, it is not art," states Kenneth F. Bates in his book *Basic Design, Principles and Practice*. Lines of confusion are most noted in contemporary styles. Fabric designs often use lines of confusion to make up printed or woven patterns.

Lines of confusion naturally occur in rainforests around the world. A combination of horizontal lines (rainforest floor), vertical lines (large trees with understory) and angled or multi-directional lines (climbing lianas and vines) exhibit chaos and no order. But, in actuality, all of the chaos and confusion is needed for the rainforest and its inhabitants to survive. Therefore, all of the elements involved work together to create balance. Disturb any element, and the balance would be destroyed.

An artist is an instrument through which the universe reveals itself.

CHAPTER 6 ...

...mposition with a distinctive mode of presentation, construction or execution. In addition to a specific style, each design takes a specific shape

...convey the message intended by the design. A design c...

...campasitian with a distinctive ...

...merous design shapes and design styles. As you study ...

relationships of lines

...styles help convey the message ...

...te a mood of celebration or solem...

...define numerous design shapes ...

...rangement of lines within each...

...parallelism, apposition, radia...

...ting a design in its pure form is the first step in creating an original campasitian...

FLOWERS TO HAVE
– HAPPENINGS BETWEEN BIRTH AND DEATH

In this chapter, we define numerous design shapes and design styles.

A design style is a composition with a distinctive mode of presentation, construction or execution. In addition to a specific style, each design takes a specific shape.

These shapes and styles help convey the message intended by the design. A design can be formal or informal. It can evoke a mood of celebration or sorrow. A design can transport us to a specific time or place.

As you study these shapes and styles, notice the arrangement of lines within each. The four universal relationships of lines (lines of parallelism, opposition, radiation and confusion) can be found in every design.

Understanding a design in its pure form is the first step in creating an original composition.

DESIGN SHAPES

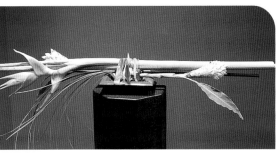

Abstract

The word abstract comes from two Latin words *abs* and *traho*, which mean 'from' and 'draw'. The word originally meant 'draw from' or 'separate'. Artists separate one or two hidden qualities from nature and try to express them. Abstract designs are not classical forms. They are balanced "free-forms" which usually exhibit non-traditional focal areas, crossing lines and focusing on color, shape and/or texture of materials.

Crescent

The shape of the design resembles a quarter moon. One of the loveliest of all shapes, it suggests movement and is derived from the circle.

Hogarth Line

Named for English artist William Hogarth (1697-1764) the shape of the design resembles an S curve. Also called the "line of beauty." In 1753 Hogarth wrote a treatise called "The Line of Beauty" and based the line on the profile of a woman's back.

Horizontal Line

The straight horizontal line is a line of rest, repose and informality. Add a wave to the tranquil horizontal line and it takes on a feeling of motion, like a rippling brook. Horizontal designs are usually designed to look the same from either side.

L-Shape

This asymmetrical arrangement is common to Western floral design. It is formed from a strong vertical line perpendicular to a horizontal line, forming a 90° angle.

Mass Design

A compact grouping of flowers in a spherical design, as opposed to a line design or stylized arrangement. Floral designers in different areas refer to them as basic colonial, Edwardian, or old fashioned bouquets.

Triangle – Symmetrical and Asymmetrical

The triangular form is represented in Renaissance, Empire and Victorian designs. There is always a focal area, and balance and proportion are a delicate blend. Triangular designs are heavily dependent on the shape and impact of the materials used.

The classical symmetrical triangle is a pure triangle in which all three sides are equal. The visual impact and balance are evenly distributed over the composition. In the asymmetrical triangle, at least one side is unequal.

Vertical Line

A vertical line is a line of strength. It stops the eye. It is a wall which holds us back. A vertical design demands attention.

Abstract Experimental Flower Design

This style leaves the traditional behind and uses other decorative materials with natural products. The shape of the flowers is at times unrecognizable through the use of special techniques such as bundling, stacking, etc. (see Chapter 7). Elementary forms such as the globe, cube and pyramid are often the basis of abstract and experimental compositions. Geometric forms, rhythm, structure, texture and tension are some of the ingredients used.

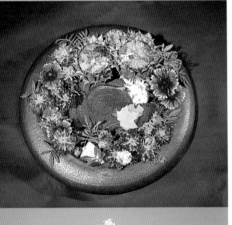

Basin (or Bowl) Design

Basin arrangements use shallow containers with materials placed slightly above or even with the container. Usually the container becomes a part of the design. Influenced by (1) the fruit bowls found in many 'still life paintings' or compote containers filled with fresh fruit used as the centerpiece on a table; or (2) the Moribana form of ikebana from the Ohara School. Basin designs are best viewed from above. Elements such as rocks, twigs or even man-made "found" items are additional sources of inspiration. The addition of water, as part of the design, helps to create an illusion of a body of water; adding an unexpected natural element to an already natural composition. Basin designs are a definite focal point in any setting.

Biedermeier

Originating in Germany and Austria as a furniture style, circa 1820-1840, this style is also a formal nostalgic compact mass of flowers and foliages. Fruits, seeds, mosses and bulbs can also be used. The materials can be arranged in various patterns:

- round, compact, concentric circles (American and Dutch style)

- pyramidal, spiral-shaped pattern (Swiss style)

- random or "salt and pepper," as in most American and Dutch style round-mass designs.

An abundance of mass materials in contrasting rows of forms and light/dark values are needed, starting at the center and working outward. Biedermeier designs are space occupying arrangements which use huge quantities of materials and exhibit romantic qualities.

Botanical Design

An American design style which features one kind of bulb plant and shows at least four parts of that plant: buds and blossoms, foliage, stems, bulb and roots. Other bulb flowers can be used in this parallel design style but are subordinate to the main flower. Botanical designs focus on the close-up look of a bulb flower.

Flobs FLORAL OBJECTS

A design style from Holland/Germany that takes on the quality of sculpture while drawing upon the classic style of the Roman/Greek era. Flobs are usually abstract experimental designs. The object, made of foliages and/or flowers, can be in any geometric shape, free-form shape or abstract shape.

Flemish

Opulent designs reminiscent of bouquets found in 15th century Dutch/Flemish paintings. Flemish painters produced magnificent floral paintings by using their artistic freedom to "cheat" on the types and seasons of flowers. They were acting as painters, flower arrangers and horticulturists. Flowers of the seasons were sketched into notebooks and these sketches were later used in large commissioned paintings.

Since there is a wide assortment of plant materials available today, it is possible to reproduce these designs. The painted arrangements were heavy and bulky, with one of everything included in them. They did not have an "arranged" look. Large flowers (tulips, lilies, crown imperials, etc.) were placed at the top because they had long stems. Small flowers with short stems were used at the bottom. There were no set rules. An important aspect of this style is a disregard for compatibility. Bulb flowers were combined with tropical flowers, fruits and other accessories for the first time. A seemingly endless variety of flowers and foliages are found in these symmetrical, massed, oval designs with the flowers facing outward, in profile, or showing their backs. Rich, varied colors, textures and many accessories (animals, insects, birds' nests, shells, fruits and vegetables) are used in these still-life groupings. These Flemish designs, like the paintings, truly display both flora and fauna.

Formal Linear

Forms and lines are dominant in this style of design. For a clear presentation of these forms and lines, the composition should be limited to a minimum of both shapes and quantities. In this style, the plant materials are portrayed through an abstracted form, surface or line. The growth movement and natural look is not a primary consideration. The formal linear design displays strong contrasting materials in which each blossom or leaf is specifically placed to assure its maximum visual importance.

Free-form
Focuses on non-geometric shapes. It embodies flowing lines, outlines and sometimes crossing lines.

Gemini
A contemporary arching system. Two separate (twin) floral designs that leap together, intermingle, connect and become one. Both designs are made of similar elements so that one transforms into another with ease.

Hedge Row or Garden Wall Design
A strict upright parallel design in which elements are aligned and massed in horizontal rows (bands) to achieve plateaus in a rich palette of colors and/ or textures. The English terminology is called Beecher's Brook.

Ikebana (Ee-kay-bah-nah)
This traditional Asian design style means "giving life to flowers." Some ikebana designs feature three main lines called shin, soe and tai (heaven, man and earth). In traditional ikebana, flower and plant materials are used as they would appear in nature, with respect for seasons, growth habitat and color harmony. Compared to Western style floral design, the container assumes more importance in ikebana designs. Various types of historical ikebana include: Rikka, Shoka, Nageire, Moribana, Free Style and Abstract.

Landscape Design

The discipline and influence of the landscape architect is seen in this style. Areas within the design are more organized, are grouped by color, and are more formal than vegetative designs. Consider using branches, garden-type flowers and basing techniques at the ground level. Using only seasonal items together in an arrangement provides a more authentic look. Taller materials are placed in the back and shorter materials are used in the front. There is little variation in the stem lengths within the same group. Staggering height differences prevent rigidity in this parallel arrangement. Stones, mosses, wood, etc. can be used as part of the base of the design.

Mille Fleur

Mille Fleur meaning "many" or "1,000 flowers" suggests that many flowers and many varieties of flowers are used. Mille Fleurs are designed principally in circular shapes; but, in contrast to the Biedermeier, the flowers are not rigid and tight, but loosely and delicately arranged. The Mille Fleurs, like the Biedermeier and Flemish, are space-occupying arrangements.

New Convention

This parallel, structured, linear design, based on the L-Shape, has strong vertical lines which are reflected with horizontal lines. Right angles (90˚) form to the front, back and sides. The New Convention design can have any number of vertical groups, although an odd number is preferable. Every medium used has a distinct personality. Each vertical line can be reflected. The reflected materials (horizontal lines) are identical to those in the vertical lines, as a tree or person standing next to a body of water is reflected horizontally in the water. There should be negative space between the strong vertical and horizontal groups. Basing techniques such as terracing, layering and clustering (see Chapter 7) using flowers, mosses, stones, leaves, etc. are important to this style. Containers used are usually low.

New Wave

The graffiti-look and playfulness of New Wave is characterized by the alteration of materials. A sculptured-looking design, flowers in this style are purposely NOT used for their natural shape, color, texture or stems. This style features discordant blends of colors and geometric shapes with unusual presentations of common products in unexpected ways depicted by the alteration (cutting, painting, gluing, etc.) of materials. Contemporary containers are necessary.

Pavé Design

Originally a jeweler's term that refers to the process of covering <u>sections</u> of a design with materials of identical size, texture and color. These materials are placed close together in irregular sections with nothing rising from the cobblestone effect. It is a flat design. While pavéing is normally used as a <u>technique</u> at the base of a design, it can be expanded into a <u>design style</u>.

Parallel-Intersection Design

A parallel arrangement has lines placed diagonally to each other in opposing directions. The most essential element is that the main lines in the design run parallel to each other respectively.

Phoenix Design

Like a fountain of water, this American style has an explosion of one material coming out the top of a tightly compact, traditional radial mass design. This style is named for the mythical phoenix bird having feathers of scarlet, blue, purple and gold. It is said to have lived for 500 years in the wilderness, then burned itself on a funeral pyre and rose from its ashes, renewed, to live again. It is an emblem of immortality and reborn hope.

Pillowing Arrangement

A compact style of designing short stemmed flowers. It is achieved by placing materials in small, irregular clusters and close together. Bunches of short flowers are joined together to form rolling hills and valleys. Some of the groups are larger or taller than the others and appear pillow-like where regular intervals are depressed.

Sheltered Arrangement

The main characteristic of this style is the placement of a roofing element hovering above the design. It is placed low, to be viewed from above and uses many basing techniques (see Chapter 7). The container becomes an important part of the design.

Spiral

Spirals, whether in animals or plants, seem to be a favored shape in nature. It can be seen in fern fronds (fiddleheads), the center of a sunflower or daisy, in pine cones, pineapples, and in many shells. It is the most forceful of all circular movements. Oddly though, this design shape has been little explored or used in creative design. In floral design, the spiral can be seen in a flat, two-dimensional shape or in a three-dimensional form. The rhythm to be found in the continued movement of the spiral can produce dynamic and interesting designs.

Topiary

Originally, it was the art of training growing plants, herbs, foliages or flowers into specific shapes ranging from animal to architectural forms. Topiaries have been adapted to formal and informal floral decorations and can be made from a variety of materials.

Vegetative Design

Flowers and/or plants designed in patterns as they would appear in nature. Overgrowth (unstructured) is the best description of this style. All materials must be compatible showing respect for the season. Using perfect, cultivated flowers will destroy the vegetative character of the arrangement. Flowers that grow straight up should not be used sideways; flowers that grow in clusters should not be used individually. Grasses, mosses, stones, driftwood and sand are ideal materials to use at the base of the design. A rustic, straight-sided container works well with this type of design.

Waterfall Design

A revival of the late 1800s romantic cascading design. Long trails of materials are needed to give the impression of flowing water. It is essential that the materials literally look as if they jump from the center of the container and cascade to the desired length. The waterfall's form and depth are created by an overlay of materials. Typical for the waterfall style is the layering of one over the other of a diversity of materials. Generally, large flowers are not used. Select smaller varieties in combination with various foliages to achieve the "untidy" appearance of a waterfall. Fresh plant materials are normally used in combination with the addition of feathers, ribbon, tulle, thread or wire as decorative elements. The first impression is that of being undisciplined, but it is one of the more difficult styles of floral design.

Western Line Arrangement

A loose triangle shaped design with a focal area near the base of the container from which all the stems appear to radiate. The graceful flowing lines are based on the classical asymmetrical triangle. The height is usually at least one and one/half to two times the width. This American style combines the lines of ikebana (Asian), with the fullness of mass design (European).

Wreath *circa 1910*
Flowers and foliages are arranged in a circular formation. In the Christian faith, it symbolizes eternity
and is used for decorations, funeral tributes or holidays.

To be remembered and nothing more, may be the secret to immortality.

CHAPTER 7 ...

Chapter 7

Techniques ar

Techniques a

ing designs Floral de

relatively essentially s

Floral design

so it is important

nique is th

It is import

everywhere. They are forming agents that connect, enhance and finish a working design. By observing these techniques one can better understa

how the components in a design relate to one another. We become inspired and mix various techniques to create a new idea or design

many different words to describe the ways they relate flowers, foliages and accessories to each other (the techniques of spacing, floral design

sign technique is the manner, means or procedure essential to transform horticultural and decorative materials into the many floral design sty

and shapes discussed in Chapter S

INSPIRATIONS FROM EARTH
—TRANSLATING TECHNIQUES INTO RESULTS

Techniques are displayed everywhere. They are forming agents that connect, enhance and finish a working design. By observing these techniques one can better understand how the components in a design relate to one another. We become inspired and mix various techniques to create a new idea or design.

Floral designers use many different words to describe the ways they relate flowers, foliages and accessories to each other (the techniques of spacing). Floral design is essentially spacing. A design technique is the manner, means or procedure essential to transform horticultural and decorative materials into the many floral design styles and shapes discussed in Chapter Six.

It is important to be familiar with the specific terms designating various techniques. The design techniques highlighted on the following pages are the details used in creating floral designs.

Baling

The tying together of many disorganized materials in an overall form (similar to a rectangular bale of hay). Baling is both functional and decorative. Materials are massed together in a disorganized fashion, tighter than in a vegetative design. There is an emphasis on the materials with interest originating in the contrasts of color, texture and variety. There are no regimented placements as in parallel designs, or natural growth patterns as seen in vegetative designs. A disorderly approach lends a sense of freedom from rules with the only boundary being the perimeter of the form. Bale the design with wire, raffia, string, bullion, or cording.

Banding

Materials surrounding a stem(s) or container for decorative purposes. It is used to accent or call attention to a particular ingredient. In its purest form it is merely a decorative item, an ornamentation, similar to a person wearing a wedding band or bracelet.

Basing Techniques

With contemporary and advanced floral designs, the ground surface or horizontal plane is arranged with intricate **textural** detail to (1) provide a decorative foundation, (2) to decoratively conceal the floral foam and mechanics, and (3) to give visual weight from which the major composition arises. Design techniques such as **bunching, clustering, layering, pavéing, pillowing** and **terracing** are often used to achieve different textural and color effects. This creates a focal interest at the base of the composition. When the basing techniques are used properly, there is space between the "base layer" and the upper materials in a composition. Basing works well with parallel system designs.

Binding

Binding physically unites several flower or foliage stems together. Binding, unlike banding, physically holds stems in place as well as being attractive.

Bunching

A labor efficient method of gathering and clustering several materials together in a bundle so that they can be placed into a design at one time. The materials in the bunch or cluster appear to radiate from a single point and are placed close to the base of the design.

Bundling

Quantities of organized materials bound together in one unit. Bundled materials can be worked into a floral design, e.g., five liatris are bound together with raffia to create one flower. New and experimental floral design uses this technique to develop more elaborate designs.

Clustering

The technique of placing like materials close together with little or no space between items. This tight grouping achieves a **mass** emphasis, maximizing the material's color, texture or shape. A cluster of grapes or the Allium giganteum inflorescence are nature's perfect examples.

Composite Flower, Composite Foliage

Constructing a large fantasy rosette flower or foliage from the petals of many smaller flowers or foliages; e.g., "glamellia"—**gla**diola petals wired or glued together to resemble a large ca**mellia**. Other composites are made from the petals of roses, gardenias, tulips, lilies, many large-leaf foliages and paper money.

Cupping

Cupping involves taking a flat, wide-leafed foliage and forming it into a cone-shaped three-dimensional object. It can be secured by gluing, stapling, or tying. Use foliages such as galax, Aspidistra, bird's-nest fern (Asplenium nidus), lily of the valley, Anthurium, Strelitzia, etc.

In most floral designs, foliage is usually of secondary importance to the flowers. With cupping, the foliage becomes an equal to the flowers. The cup may or may not be filled with another plant or object. Cupping offers separation and contrast between each flower, fruit or object placed inside. It offers support and protection, just as a bird's nest offers protection for fragile eggs. Smaller flowers (violets, Muscari, etc.), berries, fruit, eggs, cones, or Christmas ornaments are examples of items that can be placed in the cups. The stem of the flower and the stem of the foliage are usually placed together.

Detailing

Unexpected nuances that bring a superior creative flair to a design. To develop detailing skills, an artist must train his or her mind to explore possibilities for unexpected creativity.

Facing Flowers and Foliages

One of the main, but subtle, differences between Western and ikebana floral design is the way in which flowers and foliages are faced.

In Western floral design, flowers and foliages are normally faced either (1) in the same direction, or (2) in lines of radiation. Several free-form flowers (<u>Anthurium</u>, <u>Calla</u>, <u>Strelitzia</u>, <u>Spathiphyllum</u>, orchid) have definite "noses" or "directions" causing the facing of these flowers to become very obvious. If placed at the same height and faced inward on each other, "pigeon-toed," the result seems strange. In nature these flowers usually bloom on the plant in lines of radiation to take advantage of the maximum sunlight, air, and pollination. Giving direction to free-form flowers gives them order.

In ikebana floral design, the flowers' faces tend to point inward and upward, toward the sun. The flower/foliage is depicted as alive and growing. With today's instant communications and the down-sizing of our large planet into a small world, the Asian influence has reached all progressive floral designers. This "growth technique" of facing exotic, free-form flowers has been adapted by many Western artists. Likewise, foliages are handled differently. A <u>Monstera deliciosa</u> or <u>Anthurium</u> leaf might be in an arrangement with its tip facing to the left or right. Other schools of ikebana would face the leaf pointing upward, while Western design would have the leaf radiate downward from its stem.

There are other reasons for facing form flowers inward and upward such as framing and rhythm, but the ikebana way gives them unique interest and character.

Framing

The use of branches or flowers to enhance or contain other special materials. Framing isolates and calls attention to the focal area of a composition. It is also used to enclose an entire design and pull the visual impact into the design.

Grouping

A collection of floral materials separated by space from another collection of materials. Grouping is presenting materials with emphasis on color or form, joining similar items to an overall design. Distinct from bundling or bunching, the individual component parts are all visible. Grouping draws attention to the individual groups of materials and gives the colors and shapes even more strength.

Inversion/Reversal

In nature, many opposites are found in everyday situations: male-female, parent-child, husband-wife, night-day, tall-short, fat-thin, dark-light, yin-yang, etc. Chicago, noted for its outstanding architecture, has two buildings situated very close together showing inversion. The world-famous Sears Tower, like many buildings, is smaller at the top. A short distance away, the administration office of the University of Illinois, shows an unusual building designed much heavier at the top (see photo on page 69).

By using this everyday phenomena of opposites, floral design can be more interesting, and more creative. This technique can be expressed by (1) inverting the conventional shape of the design; (2) altering the placement of colors or textures; (3) inverting flowers and/or foliages.

Layering

Placing materials, usually foliages, compactly, one on top of the other so that they overlap with no space between them. Each layer is set back from the layer below it, in a stair-step fashion. Flat foliages like galax or salal are usually used. Sometimes the materials are varied and staggered in size. Layering creates a different textural effect than if the materials were used alone. For example, layering of protea or eucalyptus foliage can produce a feathery or scale-like quality.

Painting

Altering the color of a flower, foliage or container by using a commercial floral paint or floral tint. Floral paints give opaque coverage while floral tints add to the existing color.

Pavé

Pavé (pah-VAY) describes the placement of floral or non-floral items close together to cover the base of an arrangement creating a flat cobblestone effect. Most commonly used in jewelry, pavé describes the placement of identical-sized gems close together to cover the base metal. Completely pavéd jewelry shows little or no metal between the stones. In floral design, the tight placement of the materials emphasizes contrast in color and texture and has nothing emerging from the surface.

Pruning

Stripping or cutting the leaflets from foliages, or removing the florets from flowers creates voids and produces plant materials more form-like in appearance. Pruning makes the material lighter and more important looking. This Asian technique achieves an "idealized nature" as seen in bonsai and landscape-ikebana designs. Materials are pruned to show either a distant-view, mid-view, or near-view. The resulting bare stem is referred to as a "connector." The often quoted "less is more," attributed to architect Ludwig Mies van der Rohe, is a way of simplifying the plant materials for a cleaner and less complicated look.

Reflexing

Folding back the petals of a flower to give it a larger and more open effect; e.g., reflexing a rose, cymbidium orchid, tulip, or torch ginger.

Removing a Flower's Petals

Detaching some of a flower's petals results in a lighter or different looking flower; e.g., removing daisy petals evokes the notion of "she loves me, she loves me not." This technique works well with gerbera, iris, rose, and anthurium spathe; producing emotion and nostalgia for the viewer.

Rolling

Use a flat, wide-leafed foliage to form a three-dimensional roll. It can be secured by gluing and/or tying with raffia, bullion or other cording. Use foliages such as Galax, Hosta, Aspidistra, Philodendron, Anthurium or Strelitzia leaves.

Rolling is a technique where the foliage becomes almost as important as the flower. The flat foliage takes on the third dimension of depth as well as becoming a linear, tubular shape. The resulting rolls may be (1) decorative and empty, (2) used to hold and/or secure flowers, or (3) contain water tubes for holding shorter-stemmed flowers.

Sequencing

The floral materials in a design move in a natural and progressive pattern of change. The color of the flowers, the form and the size of the flowers all move in a proper sequence. Sizes move from large in the center to small on the perimeter. Colors change from darker values in the center to lighter values on the edges. Textures alter from coarse to smooth radiating out from the center. Sequencing is most forceful when there is a gradual transition in the color, in the form, or in the texture. However, it is not necessary for all three to change for the sequencing technique to be properly expressed. It is often used in creating distinctive contemporary arrangements.

Shadowing

Shadowing is the use of identical material behind and lower than the material placed in front; it is a form of repetition. It is used to give a composition a third dimension appearance by the close placement of one material immediately behind another.

Sheltering

(1) This technique creates a protected, covered feeling within or over a design. A single leaf, branches or more delicate foliages (bear grass) may partially cover or hide other materials in a design. Sheltering creates visual drama and encourages the viewer to look within to discover what is underneath.

(2) A second definition of sheltering is to keep the design within the confines of the diameter of the container, as in a vertical design and vertical container. Sheltering allows a commercial flower arrangement to be sleeved or wrapped easier and helps prevent breakage during the wrapping/delivery process.

Stacking

The process of placing the materials side by side or on top of one another. The effect is similar to a brick wall.

Stringing

The process of stringing flowers, leaves, etc., usually with needle and thread, to provide flexible garlands to use as parts of floral designs. Floral leis, commonly used in many tropical islands for decoration, are the most common form of stringing and are also probably the earliest of known floral designs.

Terracing

The horizontal positioning of flat materials to create levels or stair-steps. The placing of materials on top of each other, divided by space (as opposed to layering where there is no space in between), achieves depth with front to back placements. Terracing takes place on the container or at the container's rim.

Tufting/Pillowing

A technique of clustering or bunching materials close together at the base of a design to emphasize their color and texture. This term usually refers to clustering of rounded or dome-like materials creating small hills and valleys; e.g. roses and carnations.

Tying

A decorative accent that is achieved by forming knots with plant material which become an element within the design.

Weaving

Weaving is the process of interlacing flexible materials. Traditional weaving, usually done on a loom, consists of an upright frame within which fiber materials are interlaced vertically (the warp) and horizontally (the weft). Like prehistoric basketry, textile weaving began as a craft in the home and is universal because of its basic function (creating items that provide cover). In floral design, woven foliages are used as dimensional visual accents. Among the most used foliages are bear grass (Xerophyllum tenax), Typha, and Liriope. Any long, narrow, flexible foliage, sometimes combined with accessories such as ribbon or wire, can be used. Coconut palm, ti leaves and Pandanus have long been woven by native Hawaiian crafters.

Wrapping

The binding of large areas of floricultural items together with thread, metallic wire, fabric ribbon, yarns, etc., to add color, textural interest, and distinction to floral designs. Wrapping is distinct from banding based on size and scale.

Zoning

Zoning is a method of identifying the most space in a floral design. It is the technique of presenting important or expensive flowers in a clearly defined area of a composition, often at the top, giving them the most prominence in a design. Think of a commercial zone or residential zone taking up a large area within a city. Zoning is similar to grouping in that space must be evident between each piece of floral material. In zoning there must also be ample space between each section of materials so the flowers stand out with clear independence.

Creativity…establishing a link with Mother Nature.

CHAPTER 8 ... chapter 8

The opulent

As children bouquet holder

of a flower neatly arran

the bouquet

fragrant flo

"Aretay the end of the

called term "no

Victoria of

as Rom

below the most car

pro bouquets. To

quets of th

FLOWERS TO HOLD
_ECHOES OF HAPPINESS

As children, we view nature with curious, excited eyes. Remember how carefully we pulled each stem of a flower and clutched them together to make a bouquet to give to a loved one? This always made us happy. Little did we know that an old art of arranging flowers was being expressed.

Over the years, hand-held bouquets have had numerous purposes:
- tradition
- ethnic custom
- symbolism
- personal hygiene
- superstition/myth
- religion
- trend/fad
- personal expression

Ancient Roman brides carried small clusters of herbs as a symbol of fertility and fidelity. Greeks carried strands of ivy to their weddings as a sign of matrimony. In the mid to late 1800s, Queen Victoria of England was noted for a style of dress that was ornate and flowery. The Victorian era or Romantic era was born. Hand-held bouquets and body flowers turned from a mostly religious belief into a form of self expression. The symbolism of flowers (The Language of Flowers) was more prominent than ever. This formalness was later noted in different styles of bouquets. A special occasion was no longer needed to carry flowers. Some of the designs that became popular and that are still in use today include:
- nosegay, posey, hand-tied, clutch, tussie mussie
- cascade
- free-form
- crescent
- waterfall

The opulent Victorian era has influenced our contemporary world with numerous styles, color schemes and ornamentation. One such trademark of this era is the posey bouquet holder. It is a dainty 4" to 6" long cupped-shaped holder made of glass, ivory or metal. Silver was frequently used in its construction. The stems of flowers were neatly arranged and secured firmly in place by a pin on a chain. Below the cup, was a handle with a chain and a ring. The ring was intended to slip over a finger so the bouquet would dangle playfully during dancing. On some types, the handles open into tripod legs for standing. The practical trumpet shaped holder held delicate and fragrant flowers in two styles (1) rows of flowers in a Biedermeier style, or (2) a dotted mixture of numerous scented flowers and colors. In use from the 1830s to the end of the 1860s, these bouquets were held near the nose to encounter the nightmarish smells of European and American city streets before the age of sanitation. The term "nosegay" or "gay, happy nose" for such bouquets thus had a most practical beginning. Several imitations of these bouquet holders are available today because of their resurgence as a design trend.

The most common hand-held bouquet is the bridal bouquet used at weddings. Symbolism and superstition once played a part in the flower varieties used in making these bouquets. Today, personal expression usually prevails. From tight compact tussie mussies, to arm bouquets made of a few select flowers, to the long flowing waterfall bouquets of the Art Nouveau period, different design styles have attended our wedding ceremonies for centuries. Although design styles, flower types and color schemes have changed, the use of flowers has remained an important part of our celebrations.

Built upon a rich tradition and historic symbolism, hand-held bouquets have evolved into what we know and use today. They are echoes of the past.

circa 1900 – Victorian era. A cascade of mixed flowers with cascading ribbons. The flower girl carries a small basket of petals with blossoms.

circa 1900 – Victorian era. Bridesmaids carry walking canes wrapped with ribbon and flowers.

Cascade

1918 – Ms. Evelyn Asterbery with a clutch of roses and peonies.

Clutch

Original silver and brass Victorian nosegay holders.

Interpretive Waterfall

Free-form

Cascade

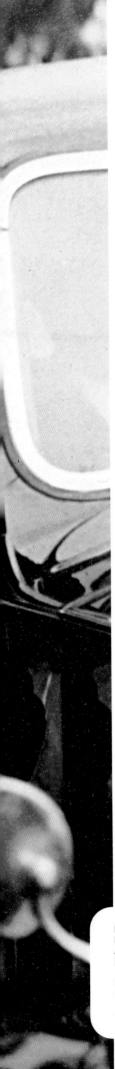

I do!

Mel and Maureen De Matoff
London, England
August 24, 1958, 2:30 p.m.
Honeymoon in Paris, France

Bridal Veil – lily of the valley
Bridal Bouquet – Crescent of white roses, lily of the valley and <u>Stephanotis</u>, with ribbon wrapped stems.

Groom – white carnation, <u>Asparagus</u> <u>plumosus</u> greenery.

AFTERWORD ...

We are living in a very fast-paced world where it seems that everything is changing at a record pace. We communicate in nanoseconds, think in megabytes and are empowered by gigawatts. Change is all around us. In nature, change is a constant; it comes with a slow deliberate and seasonal pace. While many people resist change, nature welcomes it and indeed needs this metamorphosis in order to continue. "There's something very reassuring about being able to see both the beginning and the end in the example of a plant; still more satisfying to know that the end isn't really an end at all but a kind of intermission," states Leonard Tharp in his excellent book *An American Style of Flower Arrangement.* In the reality of nature, the more things change, the more they stay the same.

If we're being totally honest, we must understand that the true purpose of a flower is to reproduce its kind; to carry on its species. The spectacular blossoms that we use so freely to communicate have a language of their own. Every sentiment and emotion is expressed in one form or another by these fragile blooms. And, as a leading psychologist states, "Flowers are a perfect replica of the human life." Planting—Growth—Bloom—Withering. In the plant world there can be no new beginnings without a definite ending. It is in the seeds and bulbs, those small vehicles of change, that link the cycles of birth and death.

Change is necessary in both nature and floral design. Change is part of what a florist sells each time they deliver floral materials. A more subtle aspect of change is within the flower itself. Spring flowers, in particular, are so poignantly beautiful partly because their beauty is so illusive and changing. They exist in time, in color, in movement. You experience them—and they are gone. Only impressions, memories and emotions linger.

The riches of knowing nature can only be appreciated by being in tune with and understanding nature. It takes a special, almost mystical, understanding to get near to the living being of a plant. During the production of this book, I never ceased to marvel at Allan Howze's sensitivity to nature and creativity, both outdoors and in the studio; his mind impatiently racing ahead two or three designs faster than his hands could possibly work. He certainly embodies Ralph Waldo Emerson's message, "In art, the hand can never create anything higher than the heart (and mind) can inspire."

–James Moretz

ACKNOWLEDGMENTS...

Acknowledgments

Many thanks to the following who supplied designs, locations or help for this book: the staffs of Gold Leaf Design Group, Inc.®, Chicago, IL, USA, American Floral Art School, Chicago, IL, USA, and Taipei Florist, Taipei, Taiwan, R.O.C.; Jeff Bradshaw AIFD; The Chicago Botanic Gardens, Glencoe, IL; Delta Garden Expo – Greenwood Leflore Council Garden Clubs; Haskell Eargle AIFD; Roger Ebert; I. Li Hsiao; Paul E. Johnson; Joanne Klappauf, Common Ground Book Distributors, Inc.; Steve Lin; Lincoln Park Conservatory, Chicago, IL; Audrey Muhl AIFD; National Garden Bureau, Downers Grove, IL; Phil Rulloda AIFD; Peter Samek AIFD; and Wili Tolentino.

A special thank you to Darren DeMatoff for his contribution of preliminary editing and special projects design/coordination. To Barbara Gilbert, *Floral & Nursery Times*, Northbrook, IL, for her trusted advice with editing. Kudos to John Bistolfo of Bark Design, Chicago, IL, for his superlative graphic design of this book.

Photographs for this book were taken throughout Illinois: Graceland Cemetery, Chicago, IL; Calvary Cemetery, Evanston, IL; Chicago Botanic Gardens, Glencoe, IL; Lincoln Park Conservatory, Chicago, IL; Village of Winnetka, Winnetka, IL. Additional photography was taken in Arizona; California; Mississippi; North Dakota; Utah; Wisconsin; Costa Rica; Puerto Rico; Taipei, Taiwan, R.O.C.; Tokyo, Japan; and Italy. Photography by James Moretz and Allan Howze.

AFS Education Center. *AFS Professional Florists Skills Seminar, Education Centerstage.* Oklahoma City, OK: American Floral Services, Inc., not dated.

Adam, Robert. *Classical Architecture: A Comprehensive Handbook to the Tradition of Classical Style.* New York, NY: Harry N. Abrams, Inc., Publishers, 1991.

Alberts, Dries. *Floral Design & Art.* Wormerveer, Holland: De Uitgeverij BV, 1986.

Anderson, Gary A. *Floral Design and Marketing.* Columbus, OH: Ohio Agricultural Education Curriculum Materials Service, The Ohio State University. 1988.

Atkins, Robert. *Art/Speak A Guide to Contemporary Ideas, Movements, and Buzzwords.* New York, London, Paris: Abbeville Press, Publishers, 1990.

Bates, Kenneth F. *Basic Design, Principles and Practice.* Cleveland and New York: The World Publishing Co., 1960.

Benz, M. *Flowers: abstract form.* Houston, TX: San Jacinto Publishing Co., 1976.

Docker, Amanda. *Armscote Manor Book of Dried Flowers.* London: Century, 1990.

Edwards, Norman De Kalb. *The Art of Flower Arrangement.* New York, NY: The Viking Press, A Studio Book, 1961.

Faulkner, Ray., Edwin Ziegfeld, Gerald Hill. *Art Today An Introduction to the Fine and Functional Arts.*, 3rd ed., New York, NY: Henry Holt and Co., 1941, 1949, 1956.

Florists' Transworld Delivery Assn. *Florist (monthly magazine) workshop manuals, workshop lectures.* Southfield, MI, not dated.

Florists' Review (monthly magazine). Design School. Topeka, KS: Florists' Review Enterprises, Inc. 1996-1998.

Foshay, Ella M. *Reflections of Nature, Flowers in American Art.* New York, NY: Alfred A. Knopf, 1984.

Gardner, Helen. *Art Through the Ages.* New York, NY: Harcourt, Brace and Co., 1926, 1936, 1948.

Gettings, Fred. *The Meaning and Wonder of Art.* New York, NY: Golden Press, 1963.

Gleim-Clark, Katie., Bob Bigham. *Elements of Design.* Southfield, MI: F.T.D. Academy of Contemporary Education, 1992.

Gombrich, E.H. *The Story of Art.* London: The Phaidon Press Ltd., 1962.

Griner, Charles. *Floriculture Designing & Merchandising.* Albany, NY: Delmar Publishers., 1995.

Harper, Bill., Jim Moretz, Frances Porterfield. *Florists' Glossary of Terms.* Topeka, KS: Florists' Review Enterprises, Inc., 1989.

Harwell, Dan. *Searching for Design with Fibonacci and Phi.* Abilene, TX: Golden Spiral Publishing, 1995.

Howze, Allan., Kathy Lamancusa. *Decorating With Silk Flowers, Colorful Arrangements to Accent Your Home.* Lincolnwood, IL: Publications International Ltd., 1993.

Hunter, Norah T. *The Art of Floral Design.* Albany, NY: Delmar Publishers Inc., 1994.

International Correspondence Schools, Inc. *Floral Design Study Units 5 and 6, Design Styles, Part I and Part II.* Scranton, PA.1992.

Kubo, Kazumasa., Gabriele Wagner-Kubo. *Florales Gestaltungs Schema.* Tokyo, Japan: Rikuyo-sha Publishing, Inc., 1996.

Larmie, Walter E. *Flower Arranging, basics to advanced design.* Englewood Cliffs, NJ: Prentice-Hall, Inc., 1980.

Lersch, Gregor. *Spannungen floristisch gelöst.* Günzburg, Germany: Appel-Druck Donau-Verlag GmbH, 1985.

Lichten, Frances. *Decorative Art of Victoria's Era*. New York and London: Charles Scribner's Sons, 1950.

McDaniel, Gary L. *Floral Design & Arrangement*. Upper Saddle River, NJ: Prentice Hall, Inc., 1996—3rd ed.

Maia, Ronaldo., Denise Otis, Consulting Editor. *More Decorating With Flowers*. New York, NY: Harry N. Abrams, Inc., Publishers, 1991.

Moretz, James. *Commercial and Creative Design*. Chicago, IL: American Floral Art School, 1987, 1997—6th ed.

Moretz, James. *Defining design—styles and techniques*. Journal of Floral Design, Vol. 1, No. 1, American Institute of Floral Designers, Baltimore, MD., 1988.

Moretz, James. *Addition to Florists' Glossary of Terms*. Focal Points, American Institute of Floral Designers, Baltimore, MD., 1994.

Moretz, James. *Posey Bouquet Holders, An Alluring Victorian Fashion*. Chicago, IL: Flowerian Publishers, 1984.

Morley, Jim. *The Professional Floral Design Manual*. Oklahoma City, OK: American Floral Services, Inc., 1989, 1995—5th ed.

Myers, Bernard S. *Understanding the Arts*. New York, NY: Henry Holt and Co., 1958.

Redbook Florist Services Educational Advisory Committee, *Advanced Floral Design*. Paragould, AR: Redbook Florist Services, 1991.

Rulloda, Phillip M., Silverio Casabar. *Tropical & Contemporary Floral Design*. Phoenix, AZ. privately published. 1989.

Scott, Robert Gillam. *Design Fundamentals*. New York, Toronto, London: McGraw-Hill Book Co., Inc. 1951.

Sutter, Anne Bernat. *New Approach to Design Principles, A Comprehensive Analysis of Design Elements and Principles in Floral Design*. Overland, MO: Sutter Publishing Co., 1967.

Syndicate Sales, Inc. *Dynamite! An Explosive Collection of Floral Designs, Instruction Manual*. Kokomo, IN: Syndicate Sales, Inc., 1987.

Teleflora, Inc. F*lowers & (monthly magazine)*. Los Angeles, CA.

Vavra, Robert. *I Love Nature More*. New York, NY: William Morrow and Co., Inc. 1990.

Weisz, Johan. *Floral-art Styles and Techniques*. Paper presented at P.F.C.I. Workshop, July 20, 1988, S.A.F. Convention, Reno, NV,

INDEX